FLYING
BACKWARDS

Also by Herbert Knapp

Did You See This?
Beating a Dead Stick

With Mary L. Knapp

One Potato, Two Potato
Red, White & Blue Paradise

FLYING BACKWARDS

1931–20—: a Life in Verse

Herbert Knapp

Girandole **Books**
New York City

Publisher's Cataloging-in-Publication data

Names: Knapp, Herbert, 1931-, author.
Title: Flying backwards 1931–20 -- : a life in verse / Herbert
Knapp.
Description: Includes bibliographical references. | New York,
NY: Girandole Press, 2017.
Identifiers: ISBN 978-0-9971646-5-7 | LCCN 2017940158
Subjects: LCSH Knapp, Herbert, 1931-. | Poetry, American.
| BISAC BIOGRAPHY & AUTOBIOGRAPHY / Literary |
POETRY / Subjects & Themes / General
Classification: LCC PS3611.N36 F49 2017 | DDC 811.6--dc23

Text is in Minion Pro
Stylized text is in Imprint MT Shadow
Book designed by Steven M. Alper

Printed in the United States of America
First Girandole edition 2017

Life can only be understood backwards, but it must be lived forwards.

Søren Kierkegaard

FOR MARY

Words are always changing like the weather,
and so are we.
And yet the language holds itself together.
And so do we.
We aren't the people that we used to be.
But you're still you, my love, and I'm still me.

CONTENTS

INTRODUCTION

Even when I told myself my life was just one damn thing after an-
other, I somehow knew there was a story to it. I just didn't know
where to find it. I wrote this memoir hoping to do so.

But why should you read it? That, I cannot say. But I know why I
read memoirs. As I've grown older I've become more interested
in truth than art. I know, of course, that memoirs aren't entirely
true. We dramatize our memories. Or we simply don't remember
what happened accurately. Nevertheless, the fact that the author
of a memoir claims it's true gives his work a different "feel." I read
it a different way from the way I read fiction. And, yes, I also read
memoirs because I'm curious about other people's lives.

This memoir is different from most in that it's written in conversa-
tional verse. I did not do this because I think of myself as "a poet,"
nor because I think my life is poetic. I did it because it would have
been harder for me to write it in prose. Prose tempts me to digress.
Writing in conversational verse forced me to focus.

Herbert Knapp
New York City

1

FLYING BACKWARDS

Although it is unusual to see
seagulls flying backwards, it is not
one of those things that only poets see.

Flying hard, the best that they could do
against that wind was not go anywhere.
Soon they were slipping backwards, yard by yard.

Then when the storm arrived, they were swept aside,
went careening high and wide through the turbulent sky,
riding the wind, while I, completely soaked,

went home, put on dry clothes, sat down and wrote,
pressing my ballpoint hard: "To Do Today…
but I couldn't go on; I was swept away

into the past where all I'd missed at the time
flickered and flared like rhyme. I wrote all night,
but not what I sat down to write.

A RIDDLE

It can be felt but not by hands.
And though it has an outside and within,
it has no weight or skin.
I've seen it, but it's never seen.
And never will its presence be announced
by bells or blinking lights on a machine.
It tells the truth; it lies; it prophesies
but doesn't make a sound.
Forever lost, it can be found
in flavors, textures, scents, and melodies,
in empty rooms, in photographs, in stones.
It isn't air, but it is everywhere,
which is to say it isn't anywhere.
It's changing constantly but can't be changed,
is part of me but is apart from me.
It haunts me, so it's like a ghost,
but it is also like a place I go
like a ghost, invisibly, to visit.
So much for what it's like and isn't.
What is it?

Answer: The past.

KANSAS CITY, MISSOURI, 1931–1952

*We spend our days as a tale that is told.…So teach us to num-
ber our days, that we may apply our hearts unto wisdom.*

— Psalm 90

*5617 Park, Kansas City, Missouri. I was born here, on the table in
our breakfast nook.*

I'M TELLING YOU

As soon as I could talk, my mother said
I must remember my address. I do.
It's Fifty-Six-Seventeen Park.
She said my number was important, too.
It's "H" then "I" (for Highland) followed by
Two, Three, Six, Eight.
The reason was so I could tell,
if I was ever lost, where I was from.
A stranger then would take my hand
and lead me home.

Okay, I'm telling you!
Just kidding. It's a joke. Relax.
I don't know anyone at that address.
And if you tried that number on the phone,
there's no way you'd get through.
All of the technology has changed.
So have the rules.
The first thing children learn today
is never talk to strangers.
We all agree, they're safer being lost.

I AM NOT MAKING THIS UP, 1936

When my kindergarten teacher, Gladys Mince,
bent down to speak to me, she made me wince.
Gigantic earrings framed her weathered face.
I daydreamed that detectives would arrest her.
To my surprise, she left at mid-semester.
But then, alas, Miss Lemon took her place.

ONE OF MY SECRET TOYS

Every Sunday after church,
we drove to Gram's for dinner, which
on Sundays came at noon instead of six.

I'd ride in back, unheard, unseen,
all buttoned up, and combed and clean,
and ready to be brave if I was hurt.

Mother said that reading in the car
would hurt my eyes,
and so I left my book behind
but read the signs as they went by

in the same order every time:
street signs, stop signs, signs in yards,
on billboards, and above the doors
of stores.

A block from Grandma's house there was a store
not closed on Sunday, closed for good.
But there was one thing left inside behind
its big show-window's dirty veil,
a sign that said: "ON SALE—
EMERGENCY NIGHTGOWNS."

And every time we passed that sign,
I wondered what kind of emergency
required a nightgown or would leave me time
to buy one and to put it on.

Then silently I'd use my father's voice
to tell myself, "Your problem, son."
It was a gift, a treasure, one
of my secret toys.

HIDING AND SEEKING

You see the It stop counting, look around,
then cautiously venture farther from the tree.
She passes the little brother who believes
that he is in the game you're playing, too,
and then she's past the bike that someone left
lying on the grass. She squints your way
but turns away, and then you're up and running.
Leaping the bike and reaching out, you shout,
      "IN FREE!"

But she ran back in, too, and says that you
were saying "Free," before you touched the tree
and anyhow that she said one-two-three
for you, but you say you were "In" before
she said your name, but she insists that you were …
"Free!" shouts someone while you're arguing.
"No fair!" the It declares, "No fair," and calls
for alle alle outs to come on in.
      She calls again.

Then down from up in, out from under, and
around whatever they were crouched behind,
children appear, and as they cross the yards
between the day and night, they stop to talk.
A boy starts spinning, staggers, falls and laughs.
A girl picks up her bike and rides around.
The little brother's found. A dog runs through
a sprinkler's waving water veil and stops
            to shiver-shake.

A big girl starts a story. It's about
this girl who has agreed to babysit:
She takes her dog along—a collie dog—
because this murderer—the radio—
it says that he's escaped/ No, not from jail—
from the Asylum for the Criminally Insane!
He's nice, you see, but sometimes he has fits,
and once he chopped his children into bits.
            So anyhow,

after the kid she's sitting's had his bath,
and he decides which story he wants read,
she stretches out beside him on the bed
then hears this thumping. Quick, she shuts the book.
Looks straight ahead. But, oh, it's just her dog.
It's underneath the bed. She reaches down.
Her hand is licked. "Come on up here," she calls.

So out he crawls and CHOP, chop, CHOP, chop. CHOPS
       them both to bits!

A mother calls. A friend gets up and goes.
Another mother calls. Before too long
you're all alone, exploring people's yards
as if you were a ghost. You stop to look.
Inside a lighted window sits a man
who doesn't know that out here in the dark
a boy is watching him and wondering
what being grown up's going to be like.
           Your mother calls

at last, and in you go. "Where have you been?"
She tucks you in and kisses you goodnight,
clicks off the light, and shuts the door. You look.
A collie's head is growing from the wall.
You call, and she returns, but doesn't light
the light. "What's wrong?" She tucks you in again.
"Are you all right?" A second kiss, and then—
It's not a matter to be understood.
           The night is good.

JUNE

The air grew dense. The morning submarined.
Mother shouted, and the bushes leaned.
Unpinning flapping sheets, we rushed about,
went in, lowered the windows, and looked out.

One last bird, a sparrow, arrowed by.

Then drops were flicked upon the window pane
the way I'd seen my mother's hand
flick them on a frying pan.

And down came the sky.

But she and I were both inside,
and we turned on the lights.

OUT ON THE SCREENED-IN PORCH

Sitting on the glider with my father
sound asleep beside her, she can see
that she no longer sees
well enough to read
the catalogue from Sears that she's
anyhow already read.

She needs to mend a shirt, to darn a sock,
to choose the coupons for her Monday shop,
to blend the yellow powder in the lard.
But first she needs to call her children in,
and get them scrubbed and into bed,
and see to it the dog is fed.

But all she does is sit, listening
to whispers from the distant boulevard,
and watching through the screen as fireflies,
followed by shadowy children, cross the yard.

HIDEOUTS

First, I'd hide behind the couch.
Then, later on, I'd crouch
inside the tunnels the spirea made,
or drape myself on branches overhead,
or crawl out of the window by my bed
and lie upon the roof. From there I could
spy unseen upon the neighborhood.

I'd hunt the messages for me I'd left
inside of hollow trees in vacant lots—
the treasures, underneath my favorite rocks.
And then there were the hours that I spent
inside a book,
wandering through "fresh woods and pastures new,"
where no one ever thought to look.

AUGUST

In August people tied their curtains back,
and went around inside their houses
wearing slips or boxer shorts.
And after dark, when they turned on the lights,
I'd see them in there as I roamed the streets,
I was twelve in nineteen forty-three
and looking for, I told myself, a breeze.

August used to slow the city down,
and from the middle of the afternoon
on through early evening we would hear
the long, rasping, overlapping sound
of the cicadas,
like steam released from safety valves,
both near and far and all around.

I thought their lonely, maddening, yearning sound
the most poetic thing in Kansas City
until I saw a row of people dressed
in bathrobes, undershirts and slippers sitting
after dark before a cheap hotel
fanning their faces, waiting,
raked by passing headlights, for a breeze.

Today I know the people striding through
the Muehlebach's lobby were poetic, too,*
but at the time, they seemed like prose to me.
They had their reasons—that was clear—
and moved in their own atmosphere,
seeing only what they'd come to see.
It wasn't me.

That was who I had been looking for,
but all I found was a cicada's husk
hooked tightly to a tree
after the bug's emergency.
It was as cloudily transparent
as certain kinds of underwear
and fragile as an August breeze.

---

*   The Muehlebach was Kansas City's premier hotel from 1915 to
1960. Now owned and restored by Marriott, it has both state and
federal historic landmark status and is still a functioning hotel.

THE REVENGE OF THE WORD

I read in the Bible where it says
that this girl's knockers are like roes,
a set of them, a pair of twins
"which feed among the lilies."
Frowning then, I look up "roes."
The dictionary says they're "deer."
And trying to imagine this, I grin.
And then I sneer.

In *Geographics,* I've seen photographs
of fillies with their dillies on display,
and I'm an expert on brassieres
as advertised by Sears.
So where, I want to know's
the similarity that they're supposed
to have to deers—or roes—especially those
eating lilies?

Asleep that night I hear, but not with ears,
music to which rows of dancing dears
that I can see, but not with eyes,
synchronize their turns and clicks and kicks,
confusing me with pleasant fears
that somehow have to do with how they're dressed.
A closer look reveals they cannot close
their shirts across the antlers on their chests.

I HOPE YOU LIKE ME

"It was as if she had an appointment to meet the rest of herself
sometime, somewhere."
                            —Willa Cather, *Song of the Lark*

"These cozy, rainy afternoons are fun,"
 she says and smiles. She waits—then nudges you.
Your distant father rumbles, "Answer, son."

You gaze at her with empty eyes. She sighs.
Your dad demands that you apologize.
Defending you, she says, "It's just a phase."

Wanting to be needed like a drug,
 she murmurs, "Can't you see you're hurting us?"
You see it coming. Here it comes. The hug.

She wants you to be good enough to eat,
 a picture-perfect treat, but all you do
is mutter when she tries to butter you.

"Oh, my, you look so nice. How 'bout a kiss?"
You sit there out of sight before her eyes
as she proceeds with her analysis.

"Oh, hon, it's good to read. We do it, too.
But if it's overdone…and, you know, you
have a tendency to overdo."

"You can confide in us. We'll help you get
anything you want, but just make sure
it's something that we know you won't regret."

"A man needs money. Have you thought of that?"
They smile the knowing smiles of journalists.
"Or do you plan to draw it from a hat?"

"Who knows best?" they ask, exchanging looks,
afraid that you are thinking you can have
the kind of life you've read about in books.

*They can't see why you won't be
the kind of person that they would have been
if their own parents had been more like them.*

*To be somebody they can recognize
the first thing you must do is to become
a stranger in their eyes.*

*I know because I'm who you're going to be.
Our story's bringing you to me.
It's true. You'll see.*

And when we get together, we'll review
the way I've always shadowed you.
I'll bet you'll say you always knew.

Disguised as people that you know,
my messengers will tell you where to go.
I hope you like me.

CONVERSATIONS

She would say, "If I've told you once,
I've told you a thousand times.
When you come in the house, take off your hat."
And I would shrug, and she would say,
"How often do I have to tell you that?"
And I would shrug, and she would say,
"Stand up straight and shut the fridge.
You're wasting cold. Tuck in your shirt.
Please and thank you are the magic words.
Put down that book. Get back to work.
For heaven's sake, a little dirt
won't hurt you. All it needs is elbow grease.
Where's your gumption? Ladies first.
Did you forget the…" "No," I'd say,
But then I'd have to ask her, "Where's it at?"
And she would say, "Before the at."
Puzzled, I would shrug and turn away.

I learned much later there were certain words
you weren't supposed to end a sentence with,
and "at" was one of them. But by that time
poets had abandoned rhyme.
and everyone was nonjudgmental.
Nobody cared where "at" was anymore.

THE SERMON

All passionate language does of itself become musical.
                                        —Thomas Carlyle

 STOP IT! You're just TRYING to be different!
"OR-din-ARy"—Oh,
 THAT'S not good enough for "US."
"WE'RE" too GOOD
 for OR-din-ARy ANy-THING!
 For "US,"
 THINGS have to be JUST SO!
 Well, son, you'll soon discover you don't know
 half as much as you're inclined to THINK.
 This old world's not going to STOP
 and turn itself completely inside OUT
 to please the likes of YOU, for heaven's sake.
 Just WHEN do you intend to take
 a LIT-Tle PLAIN re-SPON-si-BIL-iTY?
 You won't be happy till you do!
 I guess you're proud of how you're acting.
 YES, 'cause if you weren't you'd CHANGE!
 Well, doesn't it then seem STRANGE
 that no one ELSE behaves the way you do?
 Your trouble is you TALK but can't pro-DUCE!
 Nothing that's worth MONEY!
 Nothing that's of USE

and won't as long you insist
on sticking to that stuck-up attitude.
It's RUDE!
We love you, honey.

SILENTLY HE PARODIES THE PREACHER

Yes, and, son, what makes you think
you've got the talent to be minor, even?
What if all you'll do—
after you've disappointed everyone—
is fail? It isn't true
that failure doesn't matter. Oh, I know
about Van Gogh.
Ignored and poor, and definitely sick,
he made, by accident, some very pricey
things as it turned out, but there's no trick
to that. The stuff in the garage
will be worth something someday, too.
But someday, honey, we'll be gone. What's wrong
with wanting to be proud of you?
Come on! Let's show them, son!
We're as good as anyone!

THE DIVE

Bored and afraid I am not brave, I dive
and slide through nowhere, breathless, half-alive,
and half-convinced I haven't held together.

I come up gasping out of sight
and swim back with the news that I'm all right.
A friend makes some remark about the weather.

A FOOLISHNESS TO THE GREEKS

The night we drove to Moberly
my "brothers" sang and joked to hide their shame.
I dozed so they assumed that I was cool,
had done it lots of times before,
and knew the score, when actually
I didn't even know the game.

Someone shouted, "Onward to Nirvana."
The dark peeled from our hi-light beams
like skin from a banana.

We paused before the steep, wide stairs that fell
from open double doors down and stopped
before our feet
then climbed on up into the light above
that shone on shadeless (perfect?) love.

Ready to ride in briefs and halters,
women moseyed in and out of stalls
with weathered men in overalls,
and, bridle-wise, took off my pals,
till I alone was left alive
among the dying who would soon revive
and want to go before I came.
So I exclaimed, "My kingdom…"

masking my confusion
inside a pun I'd wrapped in an allusion.
The passing fancy I addressed
didn't "get it," but she understood
more of what I meant, I think,
than would have been the case
had I, as Doctor Flesch suggests,*
expressed myself in shadeless (perfect?) prose
that knows exactly what it knows
and like a bullet goes
directly to the point.

---

*   Rudolf Flesch, *The Art of Plain Talk* (1946).

THE COUNTER-CULTURE

The lunch crowd's gone, and so I draw myself
some Guatemalan mud and sit myself
just like a customer and help myself
to what remains of someone's *Daily News*.
I want to read about my pals,
AT&T, GE, and Marriott.

They occupy, like Seraphim, Thrones, and Powers,
another world but intervene
in this one where they go about unseen
unless a wizard like myself decides
to summon them.

I peep and mutter, charm my pot
with Half-n-Half and Sweet-n-Low,
I stir it slow.
So, do they come? They do.
Incorporate as Adam—women, too—
or so 'twould seem—
Sharon, Ethyl, Loral, Tiffany—
but there's no sex as we know it to these.
They get in bed together, yes, and squeeze,
but merge instead of coupling.

"So now, my friends," I say, "about my play.
A word or two from any one of you ...
Producers would be clamoring to ... No?
Okay. Well, I've got work to do."

The legal fictions fade from view,
and, faced once more with bills to pay
I stand, re-wrap my apron 'round my waist,
re-tie my strings, and then resume,
among the counter-culture's stools,
the real life of the unbelieved in.

KANSAS CITY, MISSOURI, 1952–1963

Marriage, which has been the bourne of so many narratives, is still a great beginning, as it was to Adam and Eve, who kept their honey-moon in Eden, but had their first little one among the thorns and thistles of the wilderness. It is still the beginning of the home epic—the gradual conquest or irremediable loss of that complete union, which make the advancing years a climax, and age the harvest of sweet memories in common."

—George Eliot, *Middlemarch*

406 East Ninth Street, Kansas City, Missouri. We lived in the rear apartment on the third floor. The "Spanish girls" occupied both apartments on the second.

MORE THAN I CAN SAY

Do you remember when we stopped the car,
got out and understood the morning star?
You reached back in and turned the music up
then turned to me. The next thing I knew we
were dancing down the middle of the street.

Remember now that clown we saw last week
standing on that little ball
that he directed with his feet…

You're smiling. Too extravagant? Okay,
but there was more to us when we were dan-
cing in the street beside that car beneath
the morning star as night was turning into day
than I, without extravagance, can say.

WHAT'S GOING ON?

After the show with no place to go, we walked until dawn.
Then I emptied my pockets; you dumped your purse, and
          we found we could pay
for coffee and toast. So, "Hi," said our waitress, "What's
          going on?"
What could we say? She grinned. To her, we were plain as
          day.

THE CONFORMISTS

Too warm to wait,
rebellious lovers cast aside constraint,
but once uncovered, willingly conform.

POLITENESS

People died poorer, earlier, of less,
and bigotry was like the weather. Yes,
but every age is dark. We were polite
and wandered safely through the park at night.

"We know best. Take our advice. You must
think of the future. Stop!" our parents cried.
The years lay flat, waiting to be mowed.
Sculptured lawns smelled of insecticide.

"Face the facts," they urged. We said we were.
No money. So, no car, TV, or phone.
No newspaper. We had a radio.
They groaned but left us pretty much alone.

We lived in rooms two floors above a bar—
close to our jobs but far from our parents' dreams.
The view from our two windows was into
the giant windows of a factory

where faded women fitted rags to pipes
then worked a lever causing them to swell
to Teddy bears that would in children's arms
be charmed into an almost kind of life.

Our mothers stuffed us. Were we eating right?
They couldn't see, they said, where we were heading.
Nor could we but were content to be
wise in our own eyes and out of sight.

We were sure that greatness soon would fall
into our laps, confounding those who were
predicting less delightful things for us,
but meanwhile we accepted drinks in bars

from strangers who would wave. I stayed up late
to write. My style was touch-me-not. I wrote
of things I could not wait to understand,
demanding words make sense at my command.

Your style was Davidow. You didn't write.
But you created, swelling with the weight
of someone out of sight. So it was you
who grew so quickly unobscurely great.

Fists at midnight banged our door, and boisterous
voices, suddenly abashed when I
appeared, would say, "'Scuse us, we're looking for ..."
And I would say, "Downstairs," and close the door.

Both apartments on the second floor
were rented to the so-called "Spanish girls."
When one of them came out as we went by,
we saw a maze of beds inside. So, "Hi,"

we said. She turned away without replying.
Guys heard, "Second floor above the bar,"
and came a floor too far. Across the street
there was a grocery run by George the Greek.

"Post Toasties, please," I said, and bettors heading
back to the back room grinned and stopped to watch
as George worked free a box that had grown roots.
Who could believe in us? But we delivered

life to that neighborhood. A drunk lurched up
to take your arm and help you cross the street.
A whore just coming out our building's door
to go to work as you were coming home

stepped back and held it for you. "Thanks," you said,
and started up the narrow stairs we shared
but didn't hear it close. You felt her stare
and turned to face the fact that there are times

when things have gone too far to be made right—
when nothing can be done but be polite.
She turned to go, was stepping out of sight,
when you called down the stairs to her, "Goodnight."

OFFICE CONVERSATIONS

"Got a count on that yet?"
"Let's see, ol' bud, we had a bet."
"Oh, yeah, so how'd that game come out?"
"You lost, ol' bud, by about…"
"Hey, you got a count on that yet?"

"They hired the best man in Brazil."
"The best man in Brazil!"
"How many orders do we have to fill?"
"According to his figures, we can't buy it."
"You see ol' T.K.'s off his diet?"

"Who? Again? I know, but this is twice.
And have you seen his numbers? My advice
is write the wife we're sorry that he's sick.
But, you know, yeah, don't lay it on too thick.
Then get a new guy down there double quick."

"Who's fightin' on the tube t'night?"
"I love to see those big boys—lef' 'n a right!"
"A highball never hurt nobody's heart."
"Yes, sir, which one? We'll make a chart."
"He got 'er paid for. Then she wouldn' start!"

"Hello, hello? So, whatcha doin', hon?"
"Whadya mean he didn't get it done?
 I want results not some dad blame excuse!
 Now, where were we? Oh, what's for dinner? Great.
 Well, keep 'er warm, I'll be a little late."

THE END OF SELF-RELIANCE

Swathed in Delphic self-esteem,
I babbled reams of poetry
filled with hints and glints and gleams.
Then God sent you to ask me, "What's it mean?"

So I sat down to fill my verse with sense.
I sat as still as books upon a shelf,
sure that I could will
meanings from myself.

But I discovered sense
wasn't mine to make
and whispered when I went to bed,
"Are you still awake?"

Too tired to think, I finally knew
I needed you to open up your eyes
so I could see what was impossible
for me alone to realize.

Alone, I'm always in the dark
where Helen was before she "heard"
Annie's silent voice, which let her "see"
a world that wasn't there before the word.

RELATIONSHIPS

The poetry I wrote before we met
makes no sense and yet
its nonsense underwrites our consequence.

TO MY WIFE

When they felt God observing them,
Adam and Eve discovered shame.
Thinking of you reading what I wrote,
I do the same.

Just thinking of you reading what I wrote
causes me to see it with new eyes
and makes me wonder if I've always been
a person in disguise,
who now to my dismay,
I recognize.

AN OFFENSE

As Elly dribbles out what I've spooned in,
I scoop a spoonful up off of her chin,
then wait for her to grin
so I can slip it back in.

Experts can list her genes but can't explain
the soul she radiates enchanting me
or how, more ghostly than a ghost,
her mind's emerging from her brain
or what she's come to say to me.

I can't get used to her. She's an offense
against both theory and common sense.

And then I realize that I am, too,
and so are you. Our being here is stranger
than anything we can compare it to.

LIKE A FRANTIC BIRD (ELLY)

Like a frantic bird
that's got into a room,
my daughter babbles struggling to find
words that will allow her to get out
of her mind.

3515 Warwick, Kansas City, Missouri. We lived here when Elly was born. It was a turn-of-the-century mansion, complete with solarium and a separate carriage house. We lived in the attic.

JULY (ELLY)

While Grandma stoops to snip a rose,
her "little precious" picks her nose
and holds the booger she scoops out of it
upon her fingertip
as if a butterfly had lit on it.

THE DAY THE STEP FELL

Frank took off his coat, tucked in his shirt,
and said, "Let's not get anybody hurt.
Lift your end, Harry. Mr. Knapp, hello.
Your step's a little off. Come on, let's go!"
(He manages a club in New Orleans
and owns this rooming house that my wife cleans.)

(While visiting at Harry's house next door,
he saw our tilted step and thought he'd try
to straighten it with ropes and two by fours.)
"It's dangerous that way. You push. I'll pry."
We shifted it a bit. A slit appeared.
Frank shouted, "Stop!" and stooped to squint at it.

(Somehow Frank is in cahoots with Esther,
Harry's wife. She had a lunch prepared,
and sent "her Nemi" over here to pester
them to come.) "We're almost done," said Frank.
But Harry sighed and murmured, "Can't this wait?
Let's hire it done. We're running pretty late.

Ignoring him, Frank slid a pipe in through
the slit of air as he explained, "Now if
we lift and twist, we'll slide it back in place.
Hey, Nemi, don't just stand there. Lend a hand."
Inside the house, a phone began to ring.
The step in front of me was teetering.

(Nemi is a Filipino "boy"
of forty odd—black tie that day, white coat—
whom "everyone's just dying to employ,"
though once he ran off on a cattle boat.
Harry is retired—his heart—he goes
fishing, keeps two pointers, paints, and mows.)

Sweating and unable to let go,
I cussed as Esther on flamingo legs
below a boom of bust came 'round the hedge.
"Why isn't someone answering that phone?
Am I supposed to eat this lunch alone?"
My daughter pleaded not to go to bed.

Her mother said, "Okay, no nap today."
They kissed and hugged and sat upon the floor
inside the open door to watch us work.
I watched them watch us as I pushed and tugged
and saw them whisper and saw Mary grin.
And then I heard her say, "Because they're men."

(Did I say Esther sells antiques? She does—
displays them in her house. Frank bought this place—
the neighborhood just isn't what it was—
so he'd protect her business, just in case.
You never know. And since it's right next door.)
"Oh-oh! Now Harry, *pull!* Now back. Now *more!*"

Frowning, Harry said, "I've got a hunch…"
But Frank, already reaching for his coat
as Nemi yelled, said, "Well, let's go to lunch."
And they were gone. I stood before the moat
that one end of the step had fallen in.
A pair of scuffling sparrows came and went.

Clinks and murmurs reached us through the hedge.
Mary said, "They're pouring the champagne."
Splattered by the shade, our daughter slept.
I stood there feeling silly. Mary smiled.
Then I remembered reading, God knows where,
that long ago what "silly" meant was "blessed."

417 East 37th Street, Kansas City, Missouri. We rented the first floor. The dining room served as our bedroom. Gentlemen roomers rented the second floor bedrooms. A family lived on the third floor in the old servants' quarters.

THE GHOST (SARAH)

Lying in her bed,
listening to a story being read,
she slips into the maze inside her head,
goes far away from what is being said.

Her little body's there,
but she's inside a dark and twisty lair
with just a thread of air
to lead her back into the world we share.

I know that ghosts do not exist,
and so they can't be hugged or kissed.
And no one's ever claimed a ghost could grow.
She haunts me though.

4228 Virginia, Kansas City, Missouri. This duplex was Sarah's first home. We had the first floor: three bedrooms and a porch to accommodate our growing family.

SEE, I WAS RIGHT

Mary and I were in bed talking
when she said, "What was that?
It sounded like someone's downstairs, walking!"
I said, "Old houses sometimes sound like that."
A pause. "You don't believe me?" "Yes, I do."
I knew she did—but didn't, too.

So, throwing back the covers, I got up,
and calling loudly, "Who's in here?" I clicked
light switches on and off. "Yoo-hoo," I mocked,
but then—I don't know why—
began to stop before I looked
to listen.

"See, I was right," I said, but she was sleeping.
And I, instead of getting back in bed,
walked for half that night
between the moon-dim chairs and tables keeping
watch at windows, pausing,
in spite of what I knew, to listen.

AUGUST (ELLY)

Reading to her daughter, who is ill,
Mary stops and takes a look,
then puts the book upon the window sill.

The story it contains will keep.
She curls herself into her chair,
weeps quietly a while then goes to sleep.

Later as the curtains flair
above that book upon the window sill,
I come upon them there.

The summer morning shadows them with glory
the way a reader shadows what he sees
inside a story.

BEHIND THE MOON

As soon as our guests were gone, you raced upstairs
to settle down our daughters, who
though long abed, were still awake,
while I turned the lights off.

Crossing the room, I stopped beside our books
and with my moon-grey hands began to choose
the ones I had to read again
or read at last, soon.

The stack grew taller, tilted, fell.
And as I stood there studying,
you called for me to bring up Sarah's doll.
"Where is it?" I called back.

"We think, the kitchen." So I went to look
and through the window that's above the sink
saw clouds entrained like white tops moving West
while I was stuck fast.

I JUST REPEAT WHAT'S BEING SAID

At home one daughter's crying to be fed.
The other's feverish; she stays in bed.
My wife was up six times last night.

At work I just repeat what's being said
for fear someone will see today my head
just isn't screwed on tight.

6733 Locust, Kansas City, Missouri. A three-bedroom home of our own, but not for long. An offer to teach in Panama was too good to refuse.

SATURDAY MORNING

Mid-morning. Saturday. The beds aren't made.
I'm down here on the side porch in the shade,
while out there in the sun, the grass is growing;
and off somewhere someone has started mowing.

First I pay the bills and then I write
letters that are also debts.
I fold them, stuff them into envelopes,
then lick the flaps and press them tight.

I sometimes feel as if I am myself
a letter I am writing that will be
sent someday to someone else.
And when I'm read what will he learn of me?

I sigh, then go inside
to learn what else I have to do today.
My daughters sing and quarrel and my wife
offers me a drink of lemonade.

ROSES, ROSES, ONLY ROSES

Visiting my parents, I begin
quarreling with them before I know it.
Same old stuff. We stop and start.
It goes by heart.
We come apart.

My mother sews. My father dozes.
I go in the kitchen where it's dark
to check the fridge. I want a bite
of something, but the inner light
discloses roses, roses, only roses.

I see at once: Tomorrow there's a show.
She always wins for her arrangements, which
she can count on staying put,
unlike her children who when we were told
to "Hold it" while she snapped a photograph,
would wriggle, sniff, and make a face, or laugh.

She picks her team the day before
then keeps them cold and dosed with Listerine,
so they'll look fresh. I wince and shut the door.
But if I hadn't known so much and been
so sure of what I knew, I might have seen
something more.

JANUARY

Backing out, I slide into a ditch,
spin my wheels, and see from where I sit
branches that look brushstroked on a page.
Would they if rightly read show me a way
out of this mess?

I open the trunk, take out my father's chains
and put them on. He offered them to me
when he moved up to new all-weather tires.
My feelings showed. He stiffened. I said, "Thanks."
I said it twice.

"Why can't you just be nice?" my mother asked.
I couldn't say. I wish I knew. I know
it won't be long before I disappoint her.
She's already trying to decide
where she went wrong.

My motor roars, but I go nowhere fast,
give up, get out, and am swarmed by flakes of snow
that kiss my cheeks, my eyebrows, ears, and nose.
They're fingering my clothes. My feet are cold.
I curl my toes

and trudge back up the drive against the wind
that's pressing me to stay and to become
a solid citizen whose house and car
declare his worth, the kind of man they say's
the salt of the earth.

My parents are my habit. Like a drug,
they tighten me with twisted righteousness.
When I am crowned, when money grows on trees…
The front door opens. Mary pulls me in.
She takes my coat,
pours coffee for us both, and then we talk.
We bought this house to have a place to hide,
but we've been found, and other people's dreams
are right outside. It's time
to make our break.

PANAMA, 1963–1979

The whole tendency of modern life is toward scientific planning and organization, central control, standardization and specialization. If this tendency was left to work itself out to its extreme conclusion, one might expect to see the state transformed into an immense social machine.

—Christopher Dawson, *The Historical Reality of Christianity*

The Ridge, Gamboa, Canal Zone. Walls of wood nailed to exposed studs. It was meant for a bachelor. We took the bedroom. The girls slept in the living room. We soon moved on to larger quarters but of the same type.

61

THE AMERICAN CANAL ZONE, 1904-1979

The followers of Bellamy* should come to the Zone and stay long enough to get a few pointers.
>   —George A. Miller, Prowling About Panama (1919)

The cash that we collect down here's enough
to counter the effect of years and years
of insufficient income on
our energies and powers of concentration.
Without the A/C, though, we wouldn't last.
Even pronunciation mildews fast.

The air is like a sticky balm. Our lawn
is always green. We have routines. The sea
is always calm. There's nothing wrong
and nothing to be sad or mad about.
Nothing to believe or doubt.

---

*   Edward Bellamy ("The American Marx") wrote a science fiction novel, *Looking Backward* (1888), which described a version of a socialist United States. It was phenomenally popular, both at home and abroad. Its simplified, rationalistic political arrangements appealed to both socialists and capitalists who were tired of the political controversies that are a natural aspect of any democracy. Journalists who came to the Canal Zone (1904-1979) wrote of its remarkable resemblance to Bellamy's fictitious utopia. Some hailed it as a precursor of a socialist United States; others thought it illustrated the limitations of the socialist ideal.

Remember how we snuggled when we woke,
then leaping up, threw back our heavy quilt
and shivered as we danced into our clothes,
and how before those piss-elm fires I built,
we dreamed about an earthly paradise
where nights were warm and milk was never spilt?

We found it, too. Our dreams came true down here.
Our lives are perfect. Nothing's going to change.
Everything's worked out, and yet . . . It's strange.
There's something I've begin to fear.
Every day we've less to talk about.

A 1968 LETTER FROM EDWARD BELLAMY'S SOCIALIST DREAM WORLD, WHICH CAME AS TRUE AS DREAMS CAN COME ON THE AMERICAN CANAL ZONE IN PANAMA (1904-1979)

The dream of the late Edward Bellamy is given actuality on the Zone.
—Willis J. Abbot, *The Panama Canal in Picture and Prose*
(1913)

I'm writing you from here inside this dream that is nowhere. I have no news, since nothing happens here. Each day's not just the same, but change is little but name. Don't get me wrong. It's pleasant here. The rain is warm and brief. There are no storms, no wind, no snow, no sleet. It's sunny, but we never have the kind of heat that harvesters in Kansas know. Nor are there any rich to envy, poor to pity, or resentful and ambitious men to fear. Sound good to you? That's why we're here.

I can't be certain that you still exist, since you're not here for me to poke and pinch and twist. Your letters, though, assure me that you do—or did. It takes a while for letters to get through. You write of riots and assassinations, complain that accidents upset all calculations, children suffer, innocence is scorned, incompetence rewarded, and publicity and prizes go to flashy bores. Could not a dunce design a better world than yours? I thought so once.

Although we're free from want and worry, stress and debt down here, there's something wrong. I feel unreal. This paradise makes sense, and yet…Are zoos unreal? They are. Do they make sense? They do. Say you're an animal. Now would you rather be inside a landscaped garden where you're safe, well fed, and clean, have toys to play with, time to exercise, good company, and sex, or would you rather be outside where you are free, but fearful, hunted, and diseased? The answer's obvious, and yet…

No stories here. No problems. No complaints. My carefree children suck on Chinese plums as they play mango ball. Iguanas loll above them in the elephant ear that shades our lawn. The street is speckled with the petals of the guyacans and coral showers. Such is our happy garden state. Our lives unwind in comfort as we wait—and wait.

Yesterday as I was driving home from work, a ship appeared to slide across the street ahead of me, but it was really just beyond the land upon the narrow path between the seas that is in fact a watery machine that lifts ships up and slides them though Culebra Cut then lets them down, a dream come true that now has nothing new to do and does the same thing over every day.

I stopped to watch that ship go off somewhere, its wake unrolling glints and shadows like the gestures and the patter that magicians use to hide their tricks. Then out of nowhere,

there it was: the dream. No, not of going off to find a nev-
er-never land this time—the dream of going back to find
the story that we left behind when we came here to rest in
peace—a story in which happiness can in a blink turn into
grief, and blunders into bliss—a story in which death and love
work hand in glove to bring us all to life. That's what I miss.

*718 El Prado, Balboa, Canal Zone. A concrete fourplex. Red tile roof.
We lived upstairs on the left.*

A WALK IN THE RAINFOREST

…then your eyes shall be opened and ye shall be as gods, know-
ing good and evil.

—Genesis 4:5

Roots drip from the sky.
Clutter erases thought.
Insects kiss us; vines embrace us.
Lost, we are caught.

All around us, self-reliantly,
things grow from their own rot,
like stories that are all detail
and no plot.

Is this the knowledge we were promised?
Something titters. and a shadow blinks.

We are not the people that we were.
This damp air sticks to us like fur.

The path is fading—soon will disappear.
How do we get out of here?

SEPTEMBER (SARAH)

A passing car excites a swirl
of fallen leaves, but they do not disturb
the little girl
who's walking heel to toe along the curb,

traversing an imaginary rope,
over an imaginary pit,
steadied by the hope for an unknown
blessing on the other side of it.

THE VISITOR

Once a man whose name I missed
and then was too embarrassed to insist
that he repeat shared memories with me
about the fun we used to have in school.
I hope I didn't stare but to this day
I swear I no more knew that man
than I do you.

We both pretended till he had to go
we knew each other now because
we'd known each other then, although,
long before he left, we knew
we wouldn't meet again—

and hadn't really known each other then.

CHRISTMAS COOKIES

Tears and arguments and chocolate chips
are folded in the cookies we all thought
'twould be so Christmasy for us to make.
They fill the house with fragrance as they bake.

Mary licked the spoon
and went to bed at noon.
Elly reads a book and silently
says do not touch or talk to me.

Sarah's in the living room
Playing her guitar,
singing Christmas carols and
pretending she's a star.

Our dog beseeches me to play with her.
I think of all I cannot say to her
and then of all the things I cannot scent.
I wish I understood what I resent.

JUST OUT OF SIGHT

A yawn surprises me. I shut my eyes,
I squeeze them tight then open them
and am surprised again. It's almost dark.

I fold my newspaper and sit,
wondering where the day has gone—
and the good news.

In a minute, I'll get up and go
into the other room and get the letter
I received from you two days ago.

I know what's in it. Nothing new.
You've finished what you had to do.
When you come home you'll tell me all about it.

It's just that I would like to hold your hand
and hear your voice.
In a minute, I'll turn on the light.

Until I do I'm sure
that you've come back ahead of time.
In just a minute, I'll turn on the light.

GHOSTWRITING SPEECH

Ghostwriting speech, we stroke and lace
slow revelations on white sheets.
Yesterdays arrive next week.
Everything I read is science fiction.

When you were here.
All I saw of you when we embraced
was your left ear.
Everydayness veiled your rarity.

I lived my days as if enchanted,
loved you but took you for granted.
Life went its accustomed ways
beribboned by appropriate cliches.

But since you left I see
with a counterfeiter's clarity
the great disparity between
what I can say and what you mean to me.

Enough! I'm guilty of being apart.
Come soon.
Arrest me before I write again.
I want to face the music.

WELCOME HOME

After learning that your flight was cancelled
and you were in Atlanta waiting for
a seat on Braniff,
I put the kids to bed, and as you see,
I am, myself, asleep upon the couch.

To celebrate, the girls baked you a cake.
But wait! Don't jump to a conclusion.
You will never have seen
the kitchen so clean.

Wake me when you get in. I want to be sure
by touching you that you're
not a delusion
that we have been pretending to be true
so we'd have something to look forward to.

SOUTH EGREMONT, MA, 1982–1989

A happy rural seat of various views.
> —John Milton, Paradise Lost, Book Four

McGee Road, South Egremont, Massachusetts. Three bedrooms. Radiant heating. A gazebo. Gardens. And a view of the low Berkshire mountains. But natural beauty only goes so far.

THE FOX

The house we bought had been
empty for years when we moved in.
It was too far, which was how come
we could afford it.

Touring the unmowed yard, I crossed
shadows sliding east.
No sign of man or beast.
Then one step past the hedge, I stopped.

Something had happened fast—
too fast for me. My mind
was racing like a headless chicken,
heedless, deaf, and blind.

When I regained my sight,
a plume of smoke was flowing down the slope,
had almost reached the tanglewood.
"This can't," I told myself, "be right."

So I reviewed,
searching for a clue my eyes had caught
but had escaped my mind and saw
"fox" was the word I sought.

Upright and dancing, he had been
zeroing in,
upon the tiny noises mice made passing
back and forth beneath the matted grass.

And had I not appeared, he would have leaped.
arching in mid-air, and dived,
tail to the sky,
a carnivorous drone.*

The moral of this story's not as plain
as those of La Fontaine. The hedge
I can explain. It was an edge.
But what am I to say about the mice

down there in their underworld,
unable even to imagine the
existence of another world?
And what am I to say of me—

a presence who, before I understood,
had frightened back into the tanglewood
that hairy little man with backward knees
who was dancing in the shadows sliding east?

---

* See "How a Fox Hunts Mice in the Snow" and "You're Invisible
but I'll Eat You Anyway" on YouTube.

IT WAS NOT THE WHITED AIR

It was not the "whited air"
that squinting Emerson declared
"veils the farmhouse at the garden's end."
Nor was it the "swarming swirling snow"
that brought to Whittier's troubled mind
"hints and echoes from the life behind."
And least of all was it the snow
that to a grieving Longfellow
revealed "the secret of despair."

No, the flakes I celebrate were swift
and numerous but widely spaced,
more like the ones that Robert Bridges saw
falling, falling, falling down
dreamily at night on London town.
They started late one darkish afternoon,
a silent version of that tune,
The Rustic Wedding Symphony,
by Goldmark.

Winter was beginning, bringing us,
we were old enough to know,
slush and sneezes, pills and tea,
and hours spent in front of the TV,
like cats at windows.

But after all those years we spent,
never cold or really hot,
just vaguely damp and not unhappy,
getting so we almost liked
the sweetish-sour smell of jungle rot,
losing touch but saving dough,
we leaped up at the sight of snow,
put on our newly purchased, never worn
boots and sweaters, scarves and caps and coats,
and ran outside to wave our arms and dance,
both cold and warm at once, reborn.

We walked around our garden as the snow
came calming down,
and I recalled the Jews who pled
with God for bread but got
something else instead to make it known,
their sages said,
that no one lives by bread alone.

They called it manna. Why? Because
they had no idea what it was,
and still today nobody does.

"THAT WAS CLOSE," I SAID

I drove. You dozed beside me, and the road
kept sliding up beneath the headlight beams
the way it was supposed to.

And then the deer were there, and then they weren't.
But by the time I understood
it was too late to brake

or even lift my foot. The road was back
and our career continuing as if
nothing had happened.

"That was close," I said, and you said,
"What was close?" I told you what
as I slowed down.

Our town is a New England dream
of maple trees, white houses, and a church.
"But things are not what they seem."

Half the houses here are really stores
that sell antiques. The dealers keep their signs
small enough not to spoil the picture.

And over at our picture perfect church,
our preacher leaves his Bible on its shelf.
He preaches self-esteem and mental health.

Home, we sort our mail and flip away
unopened what we're sure has not
got anything to say to us.

Those deer were simply deer, I tell myself,
not messages, and yet it's clear
that we must change our lives this year or else.

SOUTH EGREMONT

Silent sparrows flew about the yard.
The dew was gone. The shadows, drawing up.
My silent garden told me what to do.

"Kneel," it said, "and weed. Arise and prune."
Above my head, God blew away
a dandelion-seed moon.

MANHATTAN, 1990–20—

History may be formed from monuments and records; but lives may only be written from personal knowledge, which is growing less every day and in a short time is gone forever.
                    —Samuel Johnson, "Lives of the Poets."

590 West End Avenue, New York City.

ANOTHER PARADISE LOST

1. The Garden

We vowed when we retired, we'd start again
and be the people that we should have been.
We'd make a garden good enough to sign.
I slashed and burned. You worked on the design.

At dawn, from our gazebo, you'd salute
the view with sips of coffee then go through
your nursery catalogues selecting new
performers for their stamina and hue.

At dusk, I'd watch you stroll about our yard,
as dreamy as a princess in a spell,
greeting your flower friends by name in Latin,
asking them if they were doing well.

I was my own man. I dug and planted,
lived in my boots and worked as if enchanted,
hammered, weeded, watered, pruned, and mowed,
and plowed our road and driveway when it snowed.

But then one day "my man" asked "me" why "he"
was doing this. I said the lilies "we"
were planting would transfigure "him." They did.
"He" went from clean to dirty—bright to dim.

We sensed that this was not the way to live
but lacked the words to disenchant ourselves.
Our garden grew till something had to give.
We pressed against the pressure of our dream

but told ourselves we couldn't just resign,
let all this beauty go, the deer return,
and our design sink in the tanglewood.
There was a lesson that we had to learn.

2. The Departure

What "gave" was in your back. We were afraid
your spine which had been fused when you were twelve
to stop its snaking had begin to crack.
Repeated X-rays were ambiguous.

You pointed to your pain. The doctors looked
and boasted they would set the crooked straight.
"That whole procedure's terribly out of date.
We'll make you perfect. What's left to debate?"

"My pain," you said, "My pain." They finally heard,
folded their arms, and said they couldn't say
if something no machine could register
was even there, much less would go away.

"Then what's the point?" you asked. They frowned and said
that answer wasn't in their answer book,
but told each other you could rest assured
when they were through you'd have a whole new look.

They looked at us the way that experts do
when they're unanimous and self-content
and said, reproachfully, they could not see
why you were so reluctant to consent.

Leaving the doctors to their answer books,
you read your notes and then you phoned them no.
Consulting with ourselves in garden nooks,
we told ourselves that it was time to go.

3. The City

The city is a ruined garden where
rats race through castles in the air,
a place where traffic snarls, and schedules squeeze
people dry like bittersweet does trees.

A beggar followed us. He begged for change,
but not the kind that could affect his fate.
Stuck in time and locked in his routine,
he made his bed upon a pavement grate.

The city is a place where Midas men
turn everything they talk about to cash,
and heroes are paraded through the streets
to cheers that rise, then come back down as trash.

But it is also where the answers are.
We found them in the libraries we haunted,
preserved like fruit in Mason jars,
every answer but the one we wanted:

trigger-point injections, meditation,
stretching—all the old reliables.
On subways, we saw people looking for
answers in novels, newspapers, and Bibles.

4. The Lesson

The gods of the marketplace looked down on us
from walls and up from magazines. Their eyes
promised us that if we'd worship them
they would sensationalize our sorry lives.

"Be born again. Become an image of
the picture perfect life we advertise.
You'll be forever panting, moist, and young.
No one who is shopping ever dies."

"Make yourself an item, self-possessed.
Perfect yourself with surgery, toupees,
then learn from the elect how to express
yourself in unimpeachable cliches."

We turned away and found ourselves addressed
by Mystery, Uncertainty, and Doubt,
teaching us that there's a good deal more
to life than advertisers know about.

You lived with pain so long it took a while
for us to notice it was gone.
Like prisoners who find their cell unlocked,
we asked, "Is this a trick? What's going on?"

So now you volunteer at a museum
where objects "polished by some ancient hand"
survive below the city's overgrowth—
a tangle we will never understand.

Every plan we make's upset. We laugh,
do something else. The life we lead
is not what anyone would call a dream.
You make the bed; I "mow" the rug. We read

and muse about whatever made us think
that living in a picture, free from sin,
but locked in our routines would let us be
the kind of people that we should have been.

WALKING HOME

Walking home, we're shadowed by a bum
repeating like a tape, "You got some change?"
There's no escape. I give him some.
You pity him. I say, "He's free to choose.
No one's life is written in the stars.
He's got his life to live, and we've got ours."

But when you look at me, I see how we,
for better or for worse, are constantly
informing one another's lives
in ways we almost never realize
by what we do and say and by the word
that goes unsaid but not unheard.

LOOK

My father spent a year inside his den
before we drove him to a nursing home
where he would live with others all alone
until the other world would take him in.

His desk was shut; the window shades were drawn.
His phone, unplugged; he dozed on his old couch.
After lunch, he'd turn the TV on.
But animal shows were all he ever watched.

I sat with him sometimes. We didn't talk.
The graceful predators would stalk a herd.
The whatever-they-weres would run in unison.
But one was always caught and torn apart.

The camera turned it all to art, but Dad
was still all business. Art was nuts to him.
The market was too thin. The quality,
as far as he could see, was based on whim.

I thought about that little girl in Spain
who drew her father back into the dark.
Their lanterns splashed the walls with shadow-shapes
that steadied when they stopped. She looked at him.

He looked at them: the painted animals
unseen for thirty thousand years or so.
I wonder what their painters had to say
when they stepped back to stretch or mix more paint?

It wasn't Tarzan talk. I'm sure they knew
things that we've lost sight of just as we
lost sight of what they drew. But if we asked,
"Would you explain your art?" we'd draw a blank.

When Job, a businessman with business sense,
complained that God's creation made no sense,
did God explain? Do artists ever? No.
He changed Job's channel, filled his little screen

with animals whose gracefulness made sense
irrelevant. They took Job's breath away.
My father's breath was going, too.
But every now and then, he'd murmur, "Look."

GRIEF

They've come to say they feel my pain.
They echo the language of priests.
I make appropriate sounds.
Mine is the language of beasts.

I'm glad they came and wish they'd go.
Each time one of them speaks,
his words are like the beaks of birds
feasting on the deceased.

ON VISITING MY FATHER'S GRAVE

We're here remembering you—
and ourselves, too.
The people we are now, you never knew.

DEAR SIS

My false starts lie wadded on the rug.
I kick one off as I put on my coat.
Not writing's easier each day I don't.
Ashamed? Of course. But shame's my drug. I say,
"I'm so ashamed," then get on with my day.
Words are cheap, but what I have to say is
not. It's far too deep for the clichés
that go with flowers at a time like this.
What I can't say, I must keep to myself.
Dad mocks me from his photo on my shelf.
I've put this off too long. I wanted to
be right. That's something that I got from him.
I was too proud to speak imperfectly,
too weak to trust that you'd have eyes to see
the tribute that I want these words to be.
Always right, he wasn't always nice.
Too self-sufficient to believe that we
could tie our shoes, he worked until the light
was gone and kept his work in mind till dawn.
Stick tight was his advice. I've gotten worse.
Measured by the light of day, his life
wasn't news. (We paid for his obit.)
But in the light of shared experience,
I see it differently. In devious
and crooked ways, he's us and we are him.

ON DECIDING TO READ THE BIBLE

I always knew I needed food and drink
and time to be alone to look and think,
and then, belatedly, I came to see
I needed someone to believe in me,
and since you did and do, I needed you
and learned I needed you to need me, too.
I thought that was enough, but there was more.
That little question: What is it all for?
And then like others in their time of need,
I realized I had a book to read.

CICADAS

The sad, metallic cry of a cicada
comes in from a garden in the sky
eleven floors above Manhattan's streets.
I think of long ago and somewhere else,
and wonder what I'm doing here myself.

Back in '39 in Kansas City,
every August afternoon,
a dozen mindless, harsh, metallic cries,
like robots screaming,
would rise and fall from four till it was dark,

piercing, maddening, machine-like sounds,
like steam escaping through a safety valve,
both near and far and all around.
I was eight, too young, my parents' thought,
to know what they were saying.

They were saying I would lead
the same machine-like boring life
that they and all our neighbors led.
Nothing like the stories that I read.
I held my ears.

The cries would go on winding up and down
as lawns were watered in the afterlight
and then, surprised, I'd realize
that they were gone and all that I could hear
was myself think.

How strange it is to find
meanings—things we cannot touch or see—
in words composed of senseless sounds,
and even in remembered sounds
of senseless insects sounding like machines.

They speak to me of overlapping lives—
the lives of sisters, brothers, husbands, wives,
of parents and grandparents, children, pets,
of our old Plymouth, houses, money, debts,
long picnics, ancient quarrels, and regrets.

STILL GOING ON

Remember when we walked all night
like characters inside a story,
through streetlamp shadows—no one else in sight?
Our lives were a continual allegory—
that few could see
and we ourselves sometimes had doubts about.

Well sometimes when I'm up alone at dawn,
making us our coffee, juice, and toast,
I sense that morning is still going on.
It's all around me. I am my own ghost.

I try to think of some way we can be
both here and there, both then and now. I can't
but also can't deny we're haunting me.
There's more to us than logic can allow.

LEAVE THOSE DISHES FOR LATER

Leave those dishes for later.
Let's sit with what's left of the day.
Remember Wimpy, Skeezix, Andy Capp,
Moon Mullins, Brenda Starr? Remember
Terry dancing with the Dragon Lady?

And Helen, Ginny, Doris, Billie,
Lena, Peggy, Dinah, Judy, Jo?
They radioed their voices into space
like mad astronomers.
Do you recall a Sewell Avery? No?
I know the name, but it is like
an antique tool that once was used
for no one can today imagine what.

Alas, the prophets and their prophecies.
The politicians and their policies.
They said tomorrow we'd be out of oil.
They said the population would "explode."
They said the earth was going to freeze
and then that it was going to boil.
The said that coffee would ... Do you recall?
It was always something.

Remember when reporters wrote about
Cafe Society?
The Stork, The El Morocco. Brenda Frasier.
And then there was The Great Society,
devoured by The Great Bureaucracy.
Are we alone alive of those who knew
people who never once heard anyone
say "fuck" or "screw"?

It's almost dark.
Let's walk in the park
and then come home, take books to bed,
and listen with our eyes
to the voices of the dead.

AN OLD TRICK NOW

As soon as we promised
for better or worse,
she put words in my mouth;
I did the reverse.

Then we could converse
without being heard
by a hidden bug
or a tattletale bird.

Since I can't see
there's anything to it,
I can't tell you
how we do it.

We echo each other
like rhymes in a verse
that hold it together
for better or worse.

HART CRANE

At eighty-two there are a lot of things
I cannot do, but almost every day
I walk down to the river.

Today while leaning on the boardwalk's railing,
watching seagulls "dip and pivot,"
I remembered Hart Crane.

I never liked his poems much.
I doubt if I'd have liked him much.
Apparently he didn't like himself.

The sky was over everywhere.
The tide was slapping and sloshing on the rocks.
And then I remembered something else he wrote:

"As silent as a mirror is believed
  Realities plunge in silence by…"

THE DISPLAY

For years we put our wedding silver,
china, and crystal on display
only when we entertained,
but now we use them every day.

We wash and dry them, then reset the table.
in order to enjoy the way
the light will accent them
at different times of day.

It doesn't matter if we break a few.
Our children like to think they're starting new.
They order out or barbecue. Besides,
our patterns—all of them—are discontinued.

CURSIVE FOREVER!

Do girls still register their patterns?
Or has that custom gone the way
of the stick shift, and "Some Enchanted Evening"?

A clerk told Mary that a butter knife
would suit her better as a wife
than a slim, slick, silver letter opener.

The subtext, plainly understood,
was she was not the kind of girl who would
be receiving letters on a tray.

And I suspect that her advisor
might still feel that she was right,
since these days hardly anyone can write—

at least not well enough for thoughts to spill
down their arm as naturally
as water zig-zags down a hill.

We tap our messages today.
They cover our computer screens the way
hoppers used to cover Western Kansas,

eating up time, and getting in our hair,
clogging up our minds,
and causing us to swear.

The only communications
that still arrive in envelopes are bills,
advertisements, and solicitations.

Nothing beautiful or clever,
nothing that's worth saving,
maybe to be read

by others after we are dead.
However,
Mary opens all of them with her

slim, slick, silver letter opener—
keeping the faith:
"Cursive forever!"

HALF ASLEEP, I HEARD THE CLOCK

I turn the page but fall asleep
and into another story long ago
where once again I'm playing hide and seek.
The It is moving further from the tree,
and I am just about
to run in, tag up, and to shout:
"In Free!"

Eleven stories down below
an ambulance goes by with whoops and wails.

Then silence once again prevails,
but I am all awake again.
I shut my book. There is no game to win
and all the others have already been
called in.

TO EVERYTHING I'LL NEVER UNDERSTAND

*As I grow older I find more and more as a matter of actual
experience that there is a God. . . .*
                    —Rebecca West, "This I Believe."

Because I didn't know I was asleep,
I am surprised to be awake, although
I see almost at once, like Sherlock Holmes,
what happened—how my handwriting
grew loopy, loopier, and then, collapsing,
dribbled off the page.
I wipe my mouth. There's not much light out here.

Inside my house, it's black as ink.
I feel my way,
stopping and starting, stumbling, trying to think.
The chairs and tables that have disappeared
have not gone away.

Reaching the kitchen sink,
I fill a glass
and when the water overflows,
upon my hand
I wake a second time and drink
to everything I'll never understand
but keep bumping into.

JANUARY 1

Whatever we had missed, we possessed together, the precious,
the incommunicable past.
  —The character Jim Burden in Willa Cather's *My Antonia.*

As I stood by the window watching snow
translating now to long ago,
you joined me there but did not say a word.
We shared a poem neither read nor heard.

ABOUT THE AUTHOR

HERBERT KNAPP taught in both public and private high schools for 25 years. He is the author of *Did You See This?: Poems to Provoke the Politically Correct* (Girandole Books, 2016) and *Beating a Dead Stick* (Girandole Books, 2017). He and his wife, Mary, now live in New York City. They are co-authors of *One Potato, Two Potato: The Secret Education of American Children* (W.W. Norton, 1976) and *Red, White and Blue Paradise* (Harcourt Brace Jovanovich, 1984), a memoir of their years in the American Canal Zone in Panama.